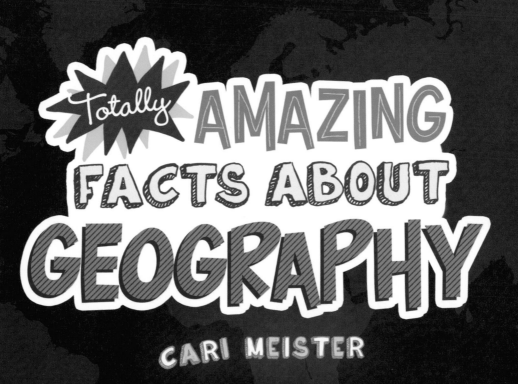

Totally AMAZING FACTS ABOUT GEOGRAPHY

CARI MEISTER

CAPSTONE PRESS
a capstone imprint

THE WORLD

THERE ARE
MORE THAN
7 billion
PEOPLE ON
EARTH.

ALL OF THEM COULD FIT IN NEW YORK CITY!

New York City

The **seven continents** cover just **one-third** of Earth's surface.

ARCTIC OCEAN

PACIFIC OCEAN

NORTH AMERICA

AFRICA

SOUTH AMERICA

ATLANTIC OCEAN

TWO-THIRDS OF EARTH'S SURFACE IS MADE UP OF OCEANS.

EUROPE

ASIA

PACIFIC
OCEAN

AUSTRALIA

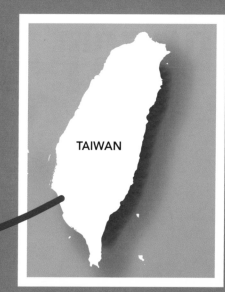

TAIWAN

There are either **195** or **196** countries in the world. Some countries don't count Taiwan.

BIGGEST COUNTRIES

CANADA

UNITED STATES OF AMERICA

#2 CANADA
3,855,103 square miles
(9,984,670 square kilometers)

#3 UNITED STATES
3,794,100 square miles
(9,826,674 sq. km)

6

RUSSIA

#1 RUSSIA

6,601,668 square miles
(17,098,242 sq. km)

LONGEST PLACE NAMES

The Welsh village of

Llanfairpwllgwyngyllgogerychwyrndrobwllllantysiliogogogoch

has one of the longest place names in the world.

Its name means: "Saint Mary's Church in a hollow of white hazel near the swirling whirlpool of the church of Saint Tysilio with a red cave."

A hill in southern Hawke's Bay in New Zealand has a really long name too:

Taumatawhakatangi-
hangakoauauotamatea-
turipukakapikimaunga-
horonukupokaiwhen-uakitanatahu

WHEN TRANSLATED, THE MEANING OF THE NAME IS:

"The place where Tamatae, the man who had big knees, the climber of mountains, the slider, the land-swallower that traveled about, played the nose flute that he had to the loved ones."

THERE ARE MORE THAN 7,000 LANGUAGES SPOKEN IN THE WORLD.

ABOUT 45 OF THEM HAVE ONLY ONE LIVING SPEAKER LEFT.

Papua New Guinea has more languages than any other country. The number? It's estimated to be about 832!

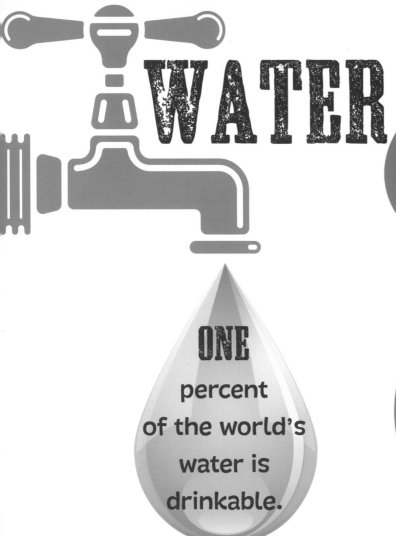

WATER

ONE percent of the world's water is drinkable.

HUNDREDS OF MILLIONS OF PEOPLE AROUND THE WORLD DO NOT HAVE ACCESS TO CLEAN WATER.

PEOPLE IN AFRICA HAVE TO WALK AN AVERAGE OF **3 miles** (4.8 KILOMETERS) TO COLLECT WATER.

13

OIL AND COAL

SAUDI ARABIA PRODUCES ONE-FIFTH OF THE WORLD'S OIL.

CHINA PRODUCES THE MOST COAL OF ANY COUNTRY. BUT IT ALSO BURNS ALMOST AS MUCH COAL AS ALL OTHER COUNTRIES COMBINED!

GOLD AND DIAMONDS

GOLD HAS BEEN FOUND ON EVERY CONTINENT.

There are **20 million** tons of gold in the ocean.

HALF OF THE GOLD MINED IS FROM SOUTH AFRICA.

Russia mines **22 PERCENT** of the world's diamonds. That's more than any other country in the world.

THE LARGEST DIAMOND EVER FOUND CAME FROM SOUTH AFRICA. IT WAS A **3,106-carat** ROCK WEIGHING **1.33 pounds** (0.6 KILOGRAMS)!

ASIA

RUSSIA

BELARUS

UKRAINE

KAZAKHSTAN

AZERBAIJAN

UZBEKISTAN

TURKMENISTAN

KYRGYZSTAN

MONGOLIA

JAPAN

NORTH KOREA

SOUTH KOREA

IRAN

TAJIKISTAN

AFGHANISTAN

CHINA

QATAR

U.A.E.

SAUDI ARABIA

OMAN

PAKISTAN

NEPAL

BHUTAN

BANGLADESH

INDIA

BURMA

LAOS

THAILAND

VIETNAM

PHILIPPINES

CAMBODIA

ANDAMAN ISLANDS (INDIA)

SRI LANKA

MALDIVES

NICOBAR ISLANDS (INDIA)

MALAYSIA

BRUNEI

MALAYSIA

INDONESIA

ASIA IS THE LARGEST CONTINENT IN AREA AND POPULATION.

18

ASIA'S LAND MAKES UP
30 percent
OF EARTH'S TOTAL LAND AREA!

The total population of Asia is
4 billion!
In fact,
60 percent
of people in the world live in Asia.

BOTH THE HIGHEST AND LOWEST POINTS IN THE WORLD ARE FOUND IN ASIA.

CHINA IS THE **FOURTH** LARGEST COUNTRY IN THE WORLD IN AREA. BUT IT HAS ONLY **ONE** TIME ZONE!

TRAINS IN INDIA ARE CROWDED. ABOUT 30 MILLION PEOPLE TRAVEL ON THEM EVERY DAY!

Japan has more than 60,000 people who are at least 100 years old!

HIMALAYA MOUNTAINS

Nine of the world's highest mountain peaks are found in the Himalayas.

THE TEMPERATURE AT THE TOP OF MT. EVEREST IS NEVER ABOVE FREEZING.

Jordan Romero climbed to the summit when he was only 13 years old!

AT MORE THAN **29,000 feet** (8,839 METERS), MT. EVEREST IS MORE THAN **10 times** TALLER THAN THE WORLD'S TALLEST BUILDING, BURJ KHALIFA!

TIBETAN PLATEAU

It's known as the

"ROOFTOP OF THE WORLD."

More than half of Asia's people get water from its glaciers.

The plateau has an average height of **16,400 feet** (4,999 m). That's more than **twice** the height of the Grand Canyon in Arizona!

CLIMATE CHANGE IS SHRINKING ITS GLACIERS.

RUSSIA

Russia is the largest country in the world. It takes up about **8.8 percent** of all land on Earth.

Pacific Ocean

Atlantic Ocean

IT IS IN BOTH ASIA AND EUROPE.

Arctic
Ocean

Russia

"It's a
long hike!"

Pacific
Ocean

Indian
Ocean

YOU COULD WALK ACROSS
RUSSIA IN ABOUT 250 DAYS
(IF YOU WALKED 8 HOURS A DAY).

Russia touches
three oceans:
the ARCTIC,
the ATLANTIC,
and the PACIFIC.

LAKE BAIKAL

RUSSIA

IT HOLDS 20 PERCENT OF EARTH'S FRESHWATER.

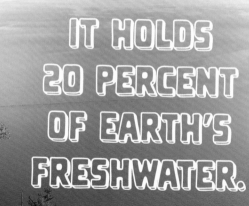

FIVE EIFFEL TOWERS STACKED ON TOP OF EACH OTHER WOULD FIT INSIDE!

This Russian lake is the deepest lake in the world, at 5,315 feet (1,620 m).

IT'S ABOUT

20 to 25 million

YEARS OLD!

THE DEAD SEA

THE DEAD SEA IS NOT A SEA. IT'S A SALT LAKE THAT LIES BETWEEN THE COUNTRIES OF ISRAEL AND JORDAN.

It's **9.6 times** saltier than ocean water!

IT IS IMPOSSIBLE FOR A PERSON TO SINK IN THE DEAD SEA.

MUMMIES FROM ANCIENT EGYPT WERE EMBALMED USING DEAD SEA MINERALS.

ZHANGYE DANXIA LANDFORM

China's "Rainbow Mountains" look like a giant multilayered cake tipped on its side!

THE LAYERS ARE MADE UP OF COLORED SANDSTONE AND MINERALS PRESSED TOGETHER.

Millions of years ago, tectonic plates caused the formation to buckle.

ZHANGJIAJIE NATIONAL PARK

CHINA

ZHANGJIAJIE WAS CHINA'S FIRST NATIONAL PARK.

IT IS HOME TO THE TALL, SKINNY TIANZI MOUNTAINS. THEY WERE THE INSPIRATION FOR THE MOVIE *AVATAR*.

At this park, you can bungee jump from a glass bridge to the canyon below.

It has an enormous glass elevator called "The Hundred Dragons Sky Lift."

MOST CROWDED CITY

TOKYO, JAPAN

Almost
38 million
people live in Tokyo.

THE AVERAGE HOME IS 750 SQUARE FEET (70 SQ. M). A SOCCER FIELD IS ABOUT 100 TIMES LARGER!

RESTAURANTS IN TOKYO ARE TINY. SOME HAVE ONLY THREE SEATS!

JEITA GROTTO

LEBANON

Under Lebanon, there is a
5.6-mile (9-km)
long group of limestone caves.

IN THE CAVES IS THE LARGEST KNOWN STALACTITE. IT IS **27 feet** (8.2 M) LONG. THAT'S TALLER THAN FIVE WOMEN STANDING ON EACH OTHER'S SHOULDERS!

Scientists discovered an ancient foundry here. They believe people made swords in the caves long ago.

SUNDARBANS

The Sundarbans is one of the largest mangrove forests in the world.

MANY ENDANGERED ANIMALS, INCLUDING THE ROYAL BENGAL TIGER, LIVE HERE.

IT IS ABOUT **541 square miles** (1,400 SQ. KM). THAT'S ABOUT HALF THE SIZE OF RHODE ISLAND.

PALM ISLANDS & WORLD ISLANDS

Dubai is famous for its manmade islands in the Persian Gulf.

THE WORLD ISLANDS ARE FOR SALE. YOU CAN BUY ONE FOR **SEVERAL** MILLION DOLLARS.

WHEN VIEWED FROM ABOVE, THEY LOOK LIKE THE WORLD.

AFRICA

AFRICA IS THE WORLD'S **second largest** CONTINENT.

Africa could hold **three** of the United States and more than **120** United Kingdoms!

People in New York City have more Internet connections than all of the people in Africa.

WITH JUST OVER **ONE BILLION** PEOPLE, AFRICA IS THE SECOND MOST POPULATED CONTINENT.

SAHARA DESERT

AFRICA

SAHARA MEANS "DESERT" IN ARABIC.

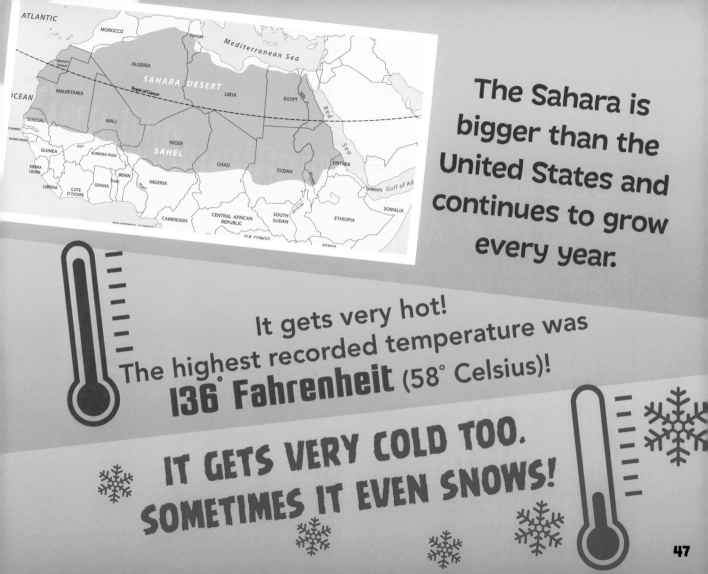

The Sahara is bigger than the United States and continues to grow every year.

It gets very hot! The highest recorded temperature was **136° Fahrenheit** (58° Celsius)!

IT GETS VERY COLD TOO. SOMETIMES IT EVEN SNOWS!

THE SERENGETI

SERENGETI COMES FROM A MAASAI WORD THAT MEANS "THE PLACE WHERE THE LAND RUNS ON FOREVER."

Disney's movie *The Lion King* was inspired by the animals of the Serengeti.

The Serengeti is famous for its incredible animal migrations. More than 1.2 million wildebeest cross it each year in search of green grass.

VICTORIA FALLS

Victoria Falls is the largest waterfall in the world (during the wet season).

LOCALS CALL IT MOSI-OA-TUNYA MEANING "SMOKE THAT THUNDERS."

ROARR!

YOU CAN HEAR THE FALLS FROM MILES AWAY.

NILE RIVER

AFRICA

At more than **4,000 miles** (6,437 km) long, the Nile is the longest river in the world.

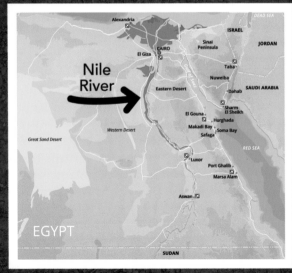

Nile River

Alexandria
CAIRO
El Giza
ISRAEL
Sinai Peninsula
JORDAN
Taba
Nuweiba
Eastern Desert
Dahab
SAUDI ARABIA
El Gouna
Sharm El Sheikh
Hurghada
Makadi Bay
Soma Bay
Western Desert
Safaga
Great Sand Desert
RED SEA
Luxor
Port Ghalib
Marsa Alam
Aswan
DEAD SEA

EGYPT

SUDAN

The famous Nile crocodiles—the largest crocs in Africa—live here. They are about 16 feet (5 m) long and weigh 500 pounds (227 kg)!

"I'm king of the Nile!"

NORTH AMERICA

NORTH AMERICA IS THE THIRD LARGEST CONTINENT.

Canada

Ottawa

United States

Washington, D.C.

Mexico

Mexico City

Nassau

Havana

Cuba

Port-au-Prince

Jamaica

Kingston

H

Belize
Belmopan

Honduras

Guatemala
City

Tegucigalpa

Guatemala

Nicaragua

San Salvador

Managua

El Salvador

Panama

San José

Panama City

Greenland

"I claimed this land for the king of Spain!"

desert

coral reef

grassland

North America has all of Earth's major biomes: desert, coral reef, grassland, tropical rain forest, and tundra.

tropical rain forest

DID CHRISTOPHER COLUMBUS DISCOVER THE AMERICAS IN 1492? MANY SCIENTISTS BELIEVE INDIGENOUS PEOPLE MOVED INTO NORTH AMERICA 15,000 YEARS AGO.

tundra

ROCKY MOUNTAINS

Apatosaurus

Stegosaurus

Allosaurus

APATOSAURUS, STEGOSAURUS, AND ALLOSAURUS FOSSILS WERE FIRST DISCOVERED ALONG THE EDGE OF THE ROCKY MOUNTAINS, IN GOLDEN, COLORADO.

THE ROCKY MOUNTAIN RANGE IS THE SECOND LONGEST IN THE WORLD.

The Continental Divide runs along the Rocky Mountains.

GREAT LAKES

LAKES HURON, ONTARIO, MICHIGAN, ERIE, AND SUPERIOR

NORTH AMERICA

THE **LARGEST** GROUP OF FRESHWATER LAKES ON EARTH IS THE GREAT LAKES.

These lakes contain more than **20 percent** of Earth's freshwater.

Lake Superior
CANADA
Wisconsin
Lake Michigan
Michigan
Lake Huron
Lake Ontario
N
Lake Erie
Pennsylva
Ohio
Ill

WATCH OUT FOR STORMS! WAVES DURING STORMS CAN REACH 35 FEET (10.7 M).

A perfectly-preserved shipwreck from 1884 lies on the bottom of Lake Superior.

GRAND CANYON

ARIZONA, UNITED STATES

Scientists do not agree on how the Grand Canyon formed.

SOME SCIENTISTS BELIEVE ITS ROCKS ARE 1 BILLION YEARS OLD.

The Grand Canyon is not the widest or deepest canyon in the world, but it is the most popular. Five million tourists visit it every year!

In one spot, the canyon is 18 miles (29 km) across.

SPOTTED LAKE

CANADA

THIS LAKE IS POLKA-DOTTED!

MINERALS IN THE WATER CAUSE THE POOLS TO CHANGE COLORS.

Native Americans have been using its healing minerals for hundreds of years.

NAICA MINE MEXICO

UNLIKE OTHER MINES (WHICH ARE COLD), THE NAICA MINE IS HOT.

MAGMA CHAMBERS UNDER THE CAVE HEAT IT TO 112°F (44°C).

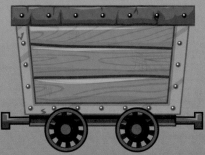

Massive beams of (selenite) crystals grow in the Naica Mine.

SOME BEAMS ARE **50 feet** (15 M) LONG AND **4 feet** (1.2 M) IN DIAMETER.

SOUTH AMERICA

SOUTH AMERICA IS THE FOURTH LARGEST CONTINENT ON EARTH.

HONDURAS
NICARAGUA
COSTA RICA
PANAMA
VENEZUELA
GUYANA
SURINAME
French Guiana
COLOMBIA
ECUADOR
PERU
B R A Z I L
BOLIVIA
South Pacific Ocean
PARAGUAY
CHILE
South Atlantic Ocean
URUGUAY
ARGENTINA
Falkland Islands (U.K.)

Besides Antarctica, it is the continent that reaches the farthest south.

The driest place on Earth is in South America. It's the Atacama Desert in Chile.

THE ANDES

At **4,500 miles** (7,242 km) long, it's the longest mountain range on land.

THE AMAZON RIVER BEGINS IN THE ANDES.

TROPICAL GLACIERS ARE FOUND HERE.

CHIMBORAZO'S PEAK IS EARTH'S CLOSEST POINT TO OUTER SPACE AND THE MOON.

AMAZON RIVER

THE AMAZON IS THE WORLD'S LARGEST RIVER BY VOLUME.

FISH CALLED ARAPAIMA ARE FOUND IN THIS RIVER. THE LARGEST ARAPAIMA EVER CAUGHT WAS 15 FEET (4.6 M) LONG AND WEIGHED MORE THAN 440 POUNDS (200 KG)!

During the wet season, the Amazon can be **30 miles** (48 km) wide!

AMAZON RAIN FOREST

The Amazon is the largest rain forest on Earth.

IT IS HOME TO MORE THAN 2.5 MILLION DIFFERENT KINDS OF INSECTS.

TWENTY PERCENT OF THE WORLD'S OXYGEN IS CREATED IN THE AMAZON.

THE TREE CANOPY IS REALLY DENSE. WHEN IT RAINS. IT TAKES 10 MINUTES FOR THE RAIN TO REACH THE FOREST FLOOR!

ANGEL FALLS

IT'S THE TALLEST
WATERFALL IN THE
WORLD. IN FACT, IT'S
15 TIMES AS TALL
AS NIAGARA FALLS
IN NEW YORK!

THE CLIFF THAT THE WATER FLOWS OVER IS CALLED AUYÁN-TEPUÍ, OR "DEVIL'S MOUNTAIN."

ANTARCTICA

IT'S COLD!
THE COLDEST TEMPERATURE ON RECORD IS -136°F (-93°C).

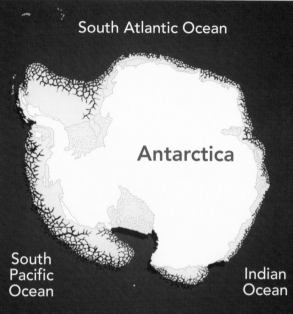

South Atlantic Ocean

Antarctica

South Pacific Ocean

Indian Ocean

ANTARCTICA CONTAINS 90 PERCENT OF EARTH'S FRESHWATER.

There is a lot of ice, but Antarctica is actually a desert. The Sahara Desert gets more rain than Antarctica!

Want to see something really cool? Throw boiling water into the air here. It instantly turns into steam or ice crystals!

EUROPE

EUROPE IS THE SIXTH LARGEST CONTINENT IN SIZE. IT'S THIRD LARGEST BY POPULATION.

ICELAND

SWEDEN

FINLAND

NORWAY

RUSSIA

ESTONIA

LATVIA

LITHUANIA

RUSSIA

BELARUS

North Atlantic Ocean

DENMARK

UNITED KINGDOM

IRELAND

NETH.

BEL.

LUX.

GERMANY

POLAND

UKRAINE

CZECH REPUBLIC

SLOVAKIA

MOLDOVA

LIECH.

AUSTRIA

HUNGARY

ROMANIA

FRANCE

SWITZ.

SLOVENIA

CROATIA

BOSNIA AND HERZEGOVINA

SERBIA

BULGARIA

MONT.

KOS.

MACE.

PORTUGAL

ANDORRA

ITALY

ALB.

TURK.

SPAIN

GREECE

Europe says:
Hi!

Hæ! Icelandic
Hei! Norwegian
Moi! Finnish
Hej! Swedish
Tere! Estonian
Haigh! Irish
Hej! Danish
Sveiki! Latvian
(Pryvitanniel) Прывітанне! Belarusian
Hi! English
Cześć! Polish
Labas! Lithuanian
(Pryvit!) Привіт! Ukrainian
Hoi! Dutch
Hallo! German
Ahoj! Czech Slovak
Salut! French
Szia! Hungarian
Bună! Romanian
Salam! Azeri
Oi! Portuguese
Zdravo! Slovenian
Zdravo! Montenegrin Bosnian
(Zdrasti) Здрасти! Bulgarian
(Voghjuyn) Ողջույն Armenian
¡Hola! Spanish
Bok! Croatian
(Zdravo!) Здраво! Macedonian Serbian
Merhaba! Turkish
Ciao! Italian
(ya!) Γειά! Greek

Europe is named after Europa, a princess from Greek mythology.

MORE THAN
250 LANGUAGES
ARE SPOKEN
IN EUROPE.

79

ALPS

The Alps stretch through Austria, Slovenia, Italy, Switzerland, Germany, and France.

THE HIGHEST POINT IS MONT BLANC,
AT **15,771 feet** (4,807 M).

MANY PEOPLE CONSIDER THE ALPS TO HAVE THE BEST SKIING IN THE WORLD.

The Alps have been home to 10 Winter Olympics.

BRITISH ISLES

The British Isles refers to two big islands (Great Britain and Ireland) and about 5,000 small islands.

Scotland

Edinburgh

Great Britain

Northern Ireland

Belfast

Isle of Man

DOUGLAS

IRELAND

DUBLIN

UNITED KINGDOM

England

Wales

Cardiff

LONDON

THERE ARE THREE COUNTRIES IN GREAT BRITAIN: ENGLAND, SCOTLAND, AND WALES.

There are more redheads in relation to total people in Great Britain than any other place on Earth.

THERE ARE HUNDREDS OF GOLF COURSES HERE. SCOTLAND ALONE HAS 550!

ICELAND

Iceland was one of the last places on Earth to be settled.

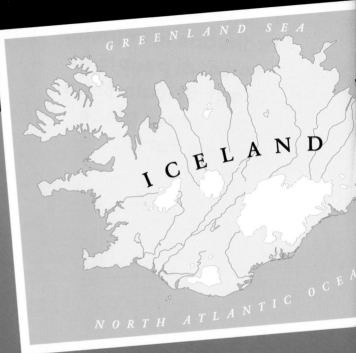

People in Iceland drink more Coca-Cola per person than in any other country.

IT IS THE LAND OF ICE CAVES-
NEW ONES FORM EVERY YEAR.

YOU CANNOT OWN A PET SNAKE, LIZARD, OR
TURTLE IN ICELAND. IT'S AGAINST THE LAW!

THE SMALLEST COUNTRY IN THE WORLD

VATICAN CITY, ITALY

VATICAN CITY IS THE SMALLEST COUNTRY IN THE WORLD.

It is about the size of Disneyland in California.

Population: about 1,000

AUSTRALIA

Australia is the smallest continent. It's about one-fourth the size of Africa.

Australia is part of an area called Oceania. Oceania includes many islands in the Pacific Ocean.

AUSTRALIA IS ALSO A COUNTRY. IT'S THE ONLY COUNTRY IN THE WORLD TO TAKE UP AN ENTIRE CONTINENT.

AUSTRALIA HAS MORE THAN 10,000 beaches.

There are more kangaroos in Australia than people.

ULURU

AUSTRALIA

IN THE MIDDLE OF AUSTRALIA SITS A MASSIVE 1,141-FOOT (348-M) HIGH SANDSTONE ROCK.

IT IS **TALLER** THAN THE GREAT PYRAMID AT GIZA AND THE EIFFEL TOWER.

IT HAS BEEN A SACRED SITE FOR NATIVE ABORIGINES FOR 10,000 years.

Some scientists believe it is **600 million** years old.

COOBER PEDY

Temperatures in Coober Pedy are hot! They're often over **120°F** (49°C).

DANGER

UNMARKED HOLES

COOBER PEDY

TO STAY COOL, 80 PERCENT OF THE POPULATION LIVES UNDERGROUND.

92

CHURCHES, BARS, AND A BOOKSTORE ARE ALSO UNDERGROUND.

Coober Pedy is the "opal capital of the world."

NINETY PERCENT OF THE WORLD'S OPALS COME FROM AUSTRALIA.

MOUNT KOSCIUSZKO

MT. KOSCIUSZKO IS AUSTRALIA'S **TALLEST** MOUNTAIN.

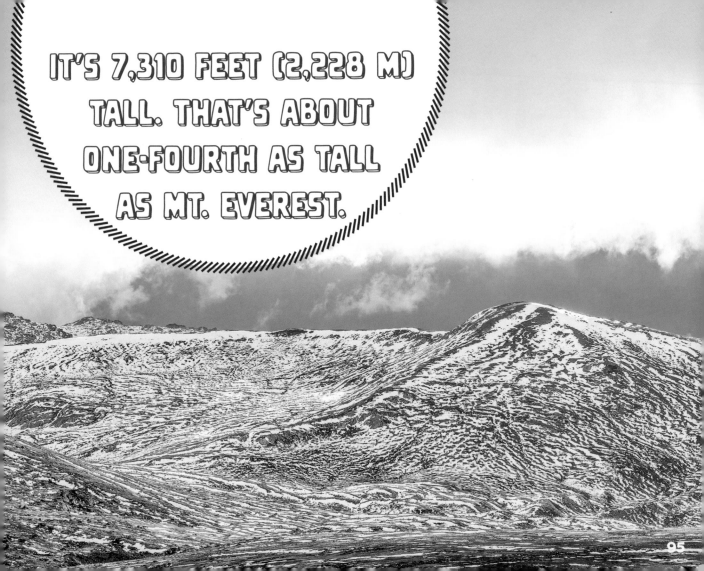

IT'S 7,310 FEET (2,228 M) TALL. THAT'S ABOUT ONE-FOURTH AS TALL AS MT. EVEREST.

95

THE OUTBACK

The "outback" refers to the parts of Australia where very few people live.

PEOPLE ESTIMATE IT COVERS ABOUT **70 percent** OF AUSTRALIA.

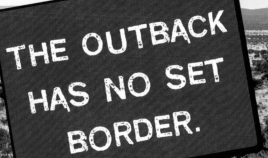

THE OUTBACK HAS NO SET BORDER.

AT CERTAIN TIMES OF THE DAY, THE OUTBACK DESERT SEEMS TO GLOW RED.

The outback is not just desert. It includes mountains, waterfalls, and beaches.

PINK LAKES

AUSTRALIA

NOT ALL LAKES ARE BLUE. SOME ARE PINK!

Lake Hillier in Western Australia looks like a giant strawberry milkshake puddle.

PINK LAKE, ALSO IN AUSTRALIA, HAS PINK SAND TOO.

SCIENTISTS ARE NOT SURE WHY SOME LAKES ARE PINK. IT'S A MYSTERY!

OCEANS

The average ocean depth is about **12,100 feet** (3,688 m).

Arctic Ocean

North America

Europe

Asia

Atlantic Ocean

Pacific Ocean

Africa

Pacific Ocean

South America

Indian Ocean

Australia

Southern Ocean

Antarctica

OCEANS COVER 71 PERCENT OF EARTH'S SURFACE.

ONLY ABOUT 5 PERCENT OF THE OCEANS HAVE BEEN EXPLORED. SCIENTISTS KNOW MORE ABOUT OUTER SPACE THAN THEY DO ABOUT OUR DEEP OCEANS.

KA-CHING!

Experts think there is about $4.5 billion of sunken treasure in the oceans!

"At least it's not lonely down here!"

There could be millions of creatures that scientists have yet to discover!

GREAT BARRIER REEF

THE GREAT BARRIER REEF IS THE **largest living structure** ON EARTH.

PACIFIC OCEAN

IT CAN BE SEEN FROM SPACE.

About 2.7 million people visit the reef every year.

MORE THAN 1,500 FISH SPECIES LIVE HERE.

MARIANA TRENCH

The Mariana Trench is the deepest known spot on Earth. It reaches almost 7 miles (11 km) under the ocean's surface.

"GHOST FISH" FROM THE APHYONIDAE FISH FAMILY

IF YOU DROPPED MT. EVEREST INTO THE TRENCH, IT WOULD BE MORE THAN 1 MILE (1.6 KM) UNDER WATER!

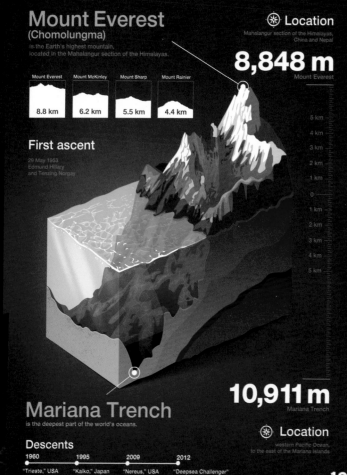

HIGHEST AND DEEPEST POINTS ON EARTH

Mount Everest
(Chomolungma)
is the Earth's highest mountain,
located in the Mahalangur section of the Himalayas.

✳ Location
Mahalangur section of the Himalayas,
China and Nepal

8,848 m
Mount Everest

Mount Everest	Mount McKinley	Mount Sharp	Mount Rainier
8.8 km	6.2 km	5.5 km	4.4 km

First ascent
29 May 1953
Edmund Hillary
and Tenzing Norgay

5 km
4 km
3 km
2 km
1 km
0
1 km
2 km
3 km
4 km
5 km

10,911 m
Mariana Trench

Mariana Trench
is the deepest part of the world's oceans.

✳ Location
western Pacific Ocean,
to the east of the Mariana Islands

Descents
1960	1995	2009	2012
"Trieste," USA	"Kaiko," Japan	"Nereus," USA	"Deepsea Challenger"

MID-OCEAN RIDGE

ABOUT 90 PERCENT OF THE WORLD'S LONGEST MOUNTAIN RANGE IS UNDERWATER.

Mid-Ocean Ridge

THE MID-OCEAN RIDGE RUNS 40,389 miles (65,000 KM).

IN COMPARISON, THE ANDES MOUNTAINS IN SOUTH AMERICA (THE LONGEST MOUNTAIN RANGE ABOVE WATER) IS 4,500 MILES (7,242 KM) LONG.

MANY OF ITS PEAKS ARE ACTIVE VOLCANOES.

BERMUDA TRIANGLE

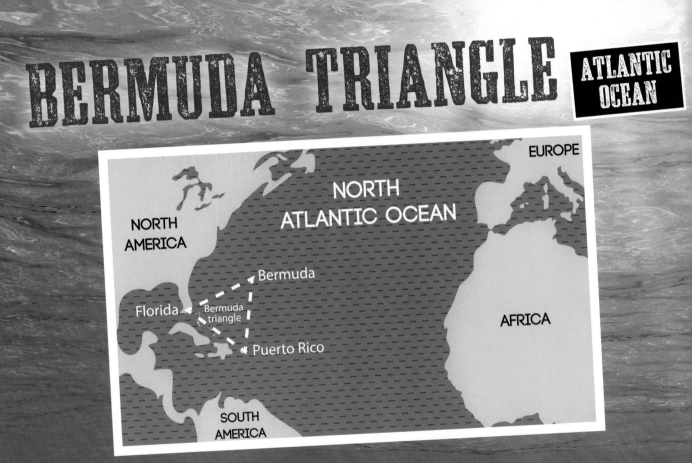

The Bermuda Triangle is a region in the North Atlantic Ocean where strange things happen.

MORE THAN 1,000 PLANES AND SHIPS HAVE DISAPPEARED WITHOUT A TRACE.

SOME PEOPLE BELIEVE THE LOST CITY OF ATLANTIS SITS UNDER THE BERMUDA TRIANGLE.

GLOSSARY

Aborigines—native people of Australia

biome—a large area on Earth containing certain types of plants

climate change—a significant change in Earth's climate over time

continent—one of Earth's seven large land masses

desert—a dry area with little rain

embalm—to preserve a dead body so it doesn't decay

glacier—a large slow-moving sheet of ice

indigenous—native to a place

magma—melted rock found beneath the surface of Earth

mangrove—a type of tree that grows along the coasts of many warm oceans and seas

migration—the regular movement of animals, usually to find food

mineral—a solid found in nature that has a crystal structure

plateau—an area of high, flat land

population—the number of people living in an area

stalactites—growths that hang from the ceiling of a cave and were formed by dripping water

tectonic plates—pieces of the Earth's crust that move around on magma

READ MORE

Meister, Cari. *Totally Amazing Facts About Stuff We've Built.* Mind Benders. North Mankato, Minn.: Capstone Press, 2017.

Really Cool People & Places: 250 Facts Kids Want to Know! Book of Why (series). New York: Time for Kids Books, 2014.

Wojtanik, Andrew. *The National Geographic Bee Ultimate Fact Book: Countries A to Z.* Washington, D.C.: National Geographic, 2012.

INTERNET SITES

Use FactHound to find Internet sites related to this book.

Visit *www.facthound.com*

Just type in 9781515777632 and go.

INDEX

Mind Benders are published by Capstone,
1710 Roe Crest Drive, North Mankato, Minnesota 56003
www.capstonepub.com

Library of Congress Cataloging-in-Publication Data
Library of Congress Cataloging-in-Publication data
is available on the Library of Congress website.
ISBN 978-1-5157-7763-2 (library binding)
ISBN 978-1-5157-7766-3 (eBook PDF)

Photo Credits: Alamy: NG Images, 43; AP Images: Binod Joshi, 23 (top right), Ekaterina Chesnokova/Sputnik, 38–39, Kamran Jebreili, 42–43, Mike Greenslade/VWPics, 93 (left), OAA Office of Ocean Exploration and Research, 104–105 (foreground), Uli Deck/picture-alliance/dpa, 16 (top left); Getty Images: Dünzl/ullstein bild, 37 (bottom); Glow Images: Jerry Kobalenko/All Canada Photos, 77, Nicolas Marino/Novarc Images RM, 24–25; iStockphoto: AarStudio, cover (bottom left), 79 (right), aeduard, 30–21, avdeev007, 28–29, Kavuto, 21, ross1248, 89, sarkophoto, 55 (bottom), sbostock, 88–89, VasjaKoman, 81; Newscom: Tim Fitzharris/Minden Pictures, 62; Science Source: Francois Gohier, 56 (left), 56 (right), Gary Hincks, 106, Javier Trueba/MSF, 65, Millard H. Sharp, 56 (middle), Science Source, 107; Shutterstock Images: 1001 craftivity, 63, 32 pixels, 24 (earth), abeadev, 48 (texture), Adwo, 67, Akura Yochi, 36–37 (background), Albert Russ, 85 (background), Alexandre Seixas, 32–33, Alexey Suloev, 76–77, Alice Nerr, 74–75, Andrzej Kubik, 45, Anna Panova, 27 (hiker), Apostrophe, 44 (background), Arsgera, 22–23, Art Berry, 52, artsandra, 40 (background), azin-v, 79 (left), badahos, 31, Bardocz Peter, 6 (Hawaii), beboy, 61, best works, 105, BGSmith, 56–57, Billion Photos, cover (top right), 101 (bottom right), blojfo, 84, Bradley Blackburn, cover (bottom right), BSVIT, 16 (top right), ChameleonsEye, 103, Christian Peters, 69 (right), creativesunday, 104–105 (background), Cvijovic Zarko, 78, Daniel Prudek, 20 (train station), David M. Schrader, 59 (top left), 59 (bottom), Dejan Popovic, 27 (footprints), Design Seed, 47 (thermometers), Designua, 100–101 (map), DongDongdog, 48–49, Dr Morley Read, 73 (insect), Edward007, 70, ekler, 18, Elena Elisseeva, 58–59, elic, 74 (background), Ella Sarkisyan, 28 (Eiffel Tower), Emdadul Hoque Topu, 40–41, Everett Historical, 54 (right), Evgeniy Dzyuba, cover (background), FiledIMAGE, 90–91, Filipe Frazao, 70–71, 72–73, Fine Art, 47 (snowflakes), Frontpage, 52–53, Galyna Andrushko, 55 (middle), Gil.K, 34, Gilles Paire, 13 (foreground), GraphicsRF, 64, graphixmania, 9 (wood sign), Greg Brave, 94–95, GTS Productions, 48, hlphoto, 93 (right), ilolab, 6–7 (background), Inga Locmele, 69 (left), ingehogenbijl, 92, Irina Klyuchnikova, 81–81, JC Photo, 102–103, Jess Kraft, 73 (right), kastianz, 68, kavram, 50–51, Ket4up, 8 (long sign), Kilroy79, 17 (background), Konrad Mostert, 99, KOSKA ill, 109 (foreground), Krasovski Dmitri, 79 (background), Laborant, 85 (foreground), len4foto, 98–99, Linda Bucklin, 109 (background), Luchenko Yana, 44 (United States), Lucky-photographer, 55 (top left), Marc Bruxelle, 72 (butterfly), Marco Saracco, 96–97, Martchan, 13 (background), MegSopki, 15 (coal), Mochipet, 32, moj0j0, 52–53 (background), 96 (background), 97 (background), NAR studio, 16 (bottom), neelsky, 40 (tiger), newelle, 90 (pyramids), Nikulina Tatiana, 74–75 (devils), Nizwa Design, 24 (water drop), npine, 15 (miner), Off Axis Production, 55 (top middle), OLOS, 35, Pasha_Barabanov, 6–7 (foreground), Patrick Foto, 82–83, peiyang, back cover (globe), 1–2 (foreground), Perati Komson, 36–37, petch one, 41 (map), Peter Hermes Furian, 28 (Russia Map), 66, 76, 82, Philip Schubert, 97 (foreground), Qvasimodo art, 10, Radu Bercan, 11, Rainer Lesniewski, 28 (Lake Baikal Map), 47 (top), 59 (top right), 84–85, Reamolko, 14, Robert Biedermann, 3, 88, rocharibeiro, cover (top left), 31 (mummy), rwgusev, 12, Ryan M. Bolton, 53, S-F, 86–87, seeyah panwan, 26–27, shockfactor.de, 51, Sophie James, 23 (bottom left), Sunny Whale, 44 (Africa), Suppapong_L, 100–101 (background), 108 (background), T. Lesia, 44 (United Kingdoms), The Adventurer, 17 (foreground), The_Pixel, 37 (top), tiptop315, 39 (blacksmith), Titov Nikolai, 90 (Eiffel Tower), TukTuk Design, 1–2 (background), Tyler Olson, 55 (top right), tynyuk, 39 (women), Vadim Sadovski, 101 (top left), Victor Z, 20 (clock), viphotos, 4–5, 20 (China), Visual society, 5, Vixit, 46, Volina, 54 (left), WAYHOME studio, 83, WindVector, 108 (foreground), xuanhuongho, 19, Yunaco, 6 (speech bubble)

Design Elements: Red Line Editorial, Shutterstock Images, and iStockphoto

SEPTEMBER 2018

Printed and bound in Canada.
010811S18